TG113504

Three Teens and a Toddler

8 Practical Tips for Moms Raising Children with an Age Gap

Mia Y Wilson

WESTBOW
PRESS®
A DIVISION OF THOMAS NELSON
& ZONDERVAN

Scripture taken from the King James Version of the Bible.

This book is a work of non-fiction. Unless otherwise
noted, the author and the publisher make no explicit
guarantees as to the accuracy of the information contained
in this book and in some cases, names of people and
places have been altered to protect their privacy.

WestBow Press books may be ordered through
booksellers or by contacting:

WestBow Press
A Division of Thomas Nelson & Zondervan
1663 Liberty Drive
Bloomington, IN 47403
www.westbowpress.com
1 (866) 928-1240

Because of the dynamic nature of the Internet, any web
addresses or links contained in this book may have changed
since publication and may no longer be valid. The views
expressed in this work are solely those of the author and do
not necessarily reflect the views of the publisher, and the
publisher hereby disclaims any responsibility for them.

ISBN: 978-1-9736-0894-3 (sc)
ISBN: 978-1-9736-0893-6 (e)

Print information available on the last page.

WestBow Press rev. date: 12/11/2017

Acknowledgements

I'm grateful for the opportunity to share just a portion of the daily tips my husband and I put into practice when raising our children. I owe the utmost respect and thanks to my husband for believing in me and encouraging me to follow my heart and choose to stay home and raise our children. It was not easy putting on hold a wonderful career as an educator that helped to support our growing family, but he encouraged me to be the woman, wife, and mother that my heart was guiding me to be in that season. I am forever grateful.

I also want to thank my mother who was one of the many women who raised children with an age gap. Mom you did a wonderful job with dad's support and I applaud your sacrifice. Thank you both for giving us our baby brother!

Lastly, I am grateful for the children that we have been blessed with. You four are the reason this book exists and I pray that these tips will be useful to you when you are parents and have your own children one day.

Mamaluv

Contents

Chapter 1

Surprise!

It had been a normal day for the family. The school week was over and the children were glad to see Friday. We ran out to grab a bite for dinner, which was a regular practice on Friday evenings in our busy household. I mean honestly, who had time to cook after handling things at home most of the week, volunteering at the school a few hours, running errands, and then doing the regular school pick-ups times three. We chose an all-you-can eat buffet that we visited often, mostly because on this night kids could eat free and since we had three, this was a deal for us. It was always a smart choice for our budget at the time. We had all scurried around the many hungry individuals, gotten our food, given thanks for the dinner, and began to eat when suddenly this flush feeling came over me. Out of nowhere, the aroma of the mouthwatering items on my plate sent an immediate feeling of nausea through my body. At first I tried to ignore it because I was so ready to enjoy a meal that I did not have to cook. Yet, the feeling remained. It was a strange combination of queasiness and a feeling of faint overcoming my body. I was a person that was rarely ever sick so this sudden feeling was not normal for me. Was there a problem with the food? Was this a stomach bug trying to ruin the meal that I was so ready for? It only took a few moments to realize that, although it had been nine years, I was all too familiar with this feeling. I immediately told my husband that I did not feel well and that we needed to leave. Of course, he and the children stuffed their mouths as quickly as they could and we headed home.

As soon as we got home I told my husband about the feeling and that I thought I was pregnant. I knew that feeling all too well as a mother of three. Little did I know that as I sat in that restaurant on that typical evening that we would welcome another little one into our family in a few months.

The next day I took a test and it was confirmed that we would soon be the parents of not only three, but four children. I can remember the feelings of surprise, shock, yet joy and thinking how our lives were about to change. We were used to life as we knew it. We no longer had cribs, diapers, baby monitors, or anything pertaining to a baby in our home. Our days were filled with afterschool sporting events, school concerts, work, our responsibilities within our local church, and pretty much a regular routine. I had just graduated with a Master's Degree and my focus was on what I wanted to do in the next season, however, in life these things happen and we trusted God as the giver of life, and we knew that everything He does is good.

After a bit of time, we told our families, our children, and of course everyone was so excited. They all knew that I loved children. Our nieces and nephews often spent so much time overnight and during the summers at our house playing and hanging out, that our home was already dubbed "Camp Wilson." Everyone figured we would handle it like pros.

While there was great excitement growing from those around us, I must make an honest admission. I had moments of wondering how this new addition to the family would affect the lives of our children, our schedules, and every-day routines. I wondered how it would all work out because this time for us it would mean literally starting over. One funny thing was that many times a commercial would come on advertising some item needed for newborns. One of our daughters would say with excitement, "Oh mom we need that for the baby!" I would calmly reply with emphasis on the word had, "We *had* that." This would happen repeatedly. The thought of having to start over with the crib, stroller, walker, high chair, the feedings, and on and on, was at times overwhelming. The thoughts of again teaching a child to walk and talk and so many other milestones that would take place was enough to send me to prayer. Don't get me wrong, I was grateful for every child my husband and I were blessed with. So many women desire to conceive and find it difficult, so I know this was another blessing from God. However, often when life as we know it is interrupted, one doesn't always immediately think of the rewards. We often think of what it will require of us instead. The one thing that really encouraged me as I processed this transition was looking back at my own mother.

My mom and dad had four children. They put a lot of time, effort, and hard work into raising us. First came my oldest brother, then I was next, and lastly was my baby sister. We were born close in age one after the other. There were family vacations, holidays, summers with grandma, childhood squabbles, and on and on. Then fifteen years later, my baby brother was born. Yes, you heard it right. There are fifteen years between my youngest brother and me. That was a true age gap, but with a lot of hard work and patience they raised him and before we knew it, he was grown and on his own. I wouldn't trade the times we had holding him, feeding him, having him visit us once we were married, and yes, even having him live with us a few times. Thinking back on the full life that my parents had traveling and doing things they enjoyed even after what seemed to be starting over, encouraged me and reminded me that I too could do it again and still have time to enjoy life with my husband once the children were raised.

Fast forward a few years after the happy arrival of our fourth child. Thankfully, everything fell into place and all the old mothering instincts kicked right back in. I was blessed to have a wonderful pregnancy and smooth delivery. The baby weighed in at 9 pounds. She was the biggest of all the others. The children were excited and my husband and I were juggling things as usual.

There were many days of siblings fussing over who would hold her, who would feed her, who would sit by her in the car seat. They enjoyed laughing as she wobbled and scooted around learning to walk. The days went by smoothly due to the excitement and the baby pretty much relied on us for everything. Thankfully, all was well and we were successfully navigating our new normal. With time passing so swiftly, it wasn't long before we found ourselves with **Three Teens and a Toddler.** Life could not have been more interesting. The smooth, calm days became filled with work, school events, church responsibilities, developmental changes, and all the normal transitions and challenges that come with raising teens. Add to this, the care of our youngest. We knew this would require a new level of focus and commitment. We also knew that with a lot of planning, and prayer, it could be done.

List a few unexpected situations that have made their way into your life.

Chapter 2

Deal with That Negative Word

For many women, a transition like this is not always such a wonderful event. It's often hard to get back into baby mode after enjoying the freedom of having self-sufficient children. Maybe you are a mom working in the corporate world and you have enjoyed working your way up the corporate ladder. Maybe you are a mother who has already raised a child or children and you were just embarking on a second career or a degree. Whatever the case, you have found yourself expecting another child and the thought of revisiting that stage of life may seem overwhelming. That brings us to our first tip which is to deal with that negative word-- regret.

It's important to know that it's okay to feel worried, concerned, unsure of yourself and even that negative word--regretful. I know that can sound harsh, but moms think with me for a moment. We as mothers and women will not say it, but there are times in our lives, when deep down inside, we may wish we would have done things differently. We wish we had planned better or taken different paths. You need to talk about those feelings, share them, pray about them, and not hold those thoughts inside. Some moms experience postpartum depression simply because they do not deal with how they are honestly feeling about their experience as a mom. There are those who want to be the perfect new mom or the super mom and they feel like they cannot live up to that challenge. Rather than sharing their regrets, insecurities, worries, doubts, and even displeasure, they keep quiet and suffer silently. It is okay to share even the deepest concerns with your mate or a trusted friend. Owning those feelings and processing them will only make for a better mommy and a more positive experience for the entire family.

If you regret revisiting this season of your life, use our first tip and deal with that feeling. Be honest, be open, let someone know how you feel so that you can get encouragement and move forward in a positive place.

How do you know if you are experiencing feelings of regret? One clue is that it's normally characterized by what you say. The Bible says, "For of the abundance of the heart the mouth speaketh." (Luke 6:45b KJV) Normally, we find ourselves talking about what we truly feel in our hearts. You may find yourself using phrases like, things were going fine before, or I feel like I'm going backwards, or I miss having my time to myself. Questions like the following may also be signs of regret: Do I have the patience to do this again? Do I have the strength to raise another child? Do I have the desire to even pour myself into this child as I did so earnestly with the others?

You will not miss heaven for thinking these thoughts or having these feelings. Realize that you are not the first mom to bring up children with an age gap and you will not be the last. Many years ago, it was common to have large families with children of varying ages. There was often a gap between the younger and the older and normally the older helped raise the younger. Now more women are choosing to work in their career fields and have children later in life, so if you find yourself starting over with children in your late 30's or 40's, you are in good company.

When my husband and I were expecting our baby almost ten years after having our others, we were actually told by one well-meaning individual, "You are supposed to be thinking about retirement and here you are having a baby". According to an article in Fortune Magazine, the National Vital Statistics Report from the Centers for Disease Control, stated that more women over age 40 are having children.[1] Another statistic states that the number of women over age 40 having babies has now overtaken those under 20 for the first time in almost 70 years.[2] Just as my husband and I realized that we were in good company, you too must know that there are many moms successfully raising children at various ages and stages of their life and so can you. You will make it. More important than any of the positive statistics, is the fact that the Bible says, "Lo, children are an heritage of the Lord: and the fruit of the womb is his reward." (Psalm 127:3 KJV) Children are a gift from God! You must choose to move forward and do as with all of life's surprises, take it one day at a time. Continually remind yourself that it is a blessing to bring a life into the world and moms are valuable.

What do you need to own, accept, and process regarding anything unexpected that has made its way into your life?

- -

- -

- -

- -

- -

- -

- -

- -

- -

- -

- -

- -

- -

- -

Chapter 3

Realize All Eyes Are on You

I f you were not exactly planning to have an additional child after your others were older, be sure to accept the transition in your heart and mind. Come to terms with the fact that this will mean another season of sacrifice. Yes, routines and schedules may have to be tweaked. Life as you knew it will need adjusting a bit, but realize that you can do it. Before making the external adjustments and changes, focus on making the internal adjustments. Begin to accept this new season in your heart and in your mind. Think about it, talk about it, see yourself in this season again. All of this is more important than running out shopping for baby things that you will need externally. Get prepared internally. Once you focus in on revisiting the season of motherhood in your heart and mind, you must then make the transition in your mouth. That means watch what you say. It's very important to have a positive outlook regarding the transition this will be for the family because the eyes of your children and family are on you. They are watching you. The family will take their cues from you. Sure, during this time there may be days when you do not feel 100% physically and emotionally, but try your best to keep all else positive.

Our children were so excited about the new baby. That is mainly because they observed our attitude and how we talked. They enjoyed looking at baby clothes and talking about names. I even had the doctor reveal the sex of the baby to them and not me so it was exciting because they knew what we were having. We were all looking forward to the baby being a part of the family. Once the baby was born, there was always competition over who would hold the baby, feed the baby, and put the baby to sleep. One would literally get upset if the other held the baby long. They loved her. She would suck her brother's face. She would blow spit bubbles and splash them when taking her bath. They loved sitting beside her in her car seat. The older children loved her, but we the parents had a lot to do with that by what we communicated verbally and non-verbally about the new baby being born into the family. She wasn't seen as drudgery. She wasn't seen as an interruption. They took their cues from us and their eyes and ears for that matter, were on us.

I remember once we took a family picture of all the grandchildren. Our older children all wanted to hold the baby. They became upset at the thought of one of the other siblings holding her for the picture. Finally, I made an executive decision and had our oldest child hold the baby. Well you should have seen a few of the faces when that picture was developed. They were not happy. All the excitement and love for their younger sister stemmed from my attitude around them. Your spouse and your children are listening and watching so keep it positive. All eyes are on you.

What do you say that you may need
to change simply because the eyes
of your children are on you?

Chapter 4

Easy Mornings Start at Night

With just a little planning, each day can be made easier for pretty much any mom but especially a mom with children having an age gap. There was a little saying that was popular around the time that we had our first two children. I kind of adopted the phrase and used it often around the house. The phrase was, "A place for everything and everything in its place". I am not sure who coined the phrase, but my children heard it often when they were young especially at night before bedtime. I firmly believe that easy mornings begin at night. I learned this tip early on after we began having children.

I was already the type of person who could barely function if things were not in order, but having children helped me kick it up a notch. Now I must say before moving on that this is not a priority for every mom. Some individuals function better by just winging it or going with the flow. However, if you are looking for help managing day-to-day responsibilities when raising children of different ages this tip will help you.

I made a practice of straightening up things in the evening before bed. Yes, like most moms I was beat by the end of the day, but this simple tip helped me to start each day without waking up to clutter and things I had to step over and navigate around. Over time it simply became routine. At night, I would have the children pick up their toys and return them to the toybox. They would place stuffed animals in their spot and they would make sure all books, games, and any miscellaneous items were returned to their places. Shoes were placed back in the closet or by the door, other items were placed on shelves, and trash was thrown away. This was so helpful because when we got up in the morning, the rooms were not filled with clutter. It just helped to start each day with a clear, fresh mind and not feel overwhelmed with chores as soon as you stepped out of bed. Even as the children got older, laptops, school textbooks, snack wrappers, cups, magazines, all had to be placed in their rooms, the kitchen, or wherever they belonged as they got up to head to bed. They would place pillows and any throw blankets back on the couch. Items were not left lying around in the family room. This may seem simple, but if you had three teens and a toddler, and everyone left all the things they were using laying around each night, you would wake up to stuff everywhere. This tip will prove helpful no matter what ages your children are and whether you are a mother working outside of the home or in the home.

Now I must admit, the older they get, reminders may often be necessary, but this is a valuable tip to put into practice. If a younger baby is involved, this means making sure all diapers are discarded, all bottles are put away, dirty bibs and soiled clothes are in the hamper, and the room is fresh and clean in the morning. I would even make sure dishes were loaded into the dishwasher. If not washed, they were at least loaded and out of sight for the next morning. Thank God for dishwashers. This may seem like a lot to do at night, but if you have children it is not. They are able to gather up their own things which leaves just a few things for you or your husband to put away. Trust me, things will flow much more smoothly each morning if the area is clutter-free the night before. More on this in the next tip.

What can be put away in your home each night to make for a more clutter-free morning?

Chapter 5

Organization and Routine-Don't Raise Kids Without Them!

Remember the saying that I mentioned in the last chapter, "A place for everything and everything in its place?" Well that saying is not just for the children. As a mom, organization and routine were extremely helpful when raising our first three children who were all about two years apart in age and especially the fourth who was born almost ten years later. They are a mom's two best friends. Whether working outside of the home, or full time in the home, (and to be honest most moms do both), organization and routine are important. We use them in corporate settings and in so many other areas so why not at home.

Let's look at organization first. Organization helps to bring efficiency and order to the home. Having designated areas in the home to store supplies, toys, books, etc. are valuable. These areas will save so much time and keep parents and children from hunting around to find things. Pretty much anything can be kept in an organized manner. No that does not mean that things are never all over the place. There are days when there may be almost chaos, but with a little organization, those days will be few.

If you are raising children with an age gap, getting organized will be of great help. One example of organization that was helpful for us with our children happened almost every night during school season. The children knew that every day when homework was completed, it had to be placed in the proper folder and in the book bag. Notebooks were not left lying around. Once all work was completed, book bags had to be packed and by the door each night. Any papers that needed to be signed for school were signed the night before, placed in the proper folder, and then placed in the book bag by the door. We did not get up hunting around for papers or homework on school mornings. This organization helped to ensure that they would know where all of their school things were each morning, and they would not get to school and realize they had left something at home. We had three teens driving to school and a younger child being dropped off at pre-school. To get that done daily without anyone leaving anything required organization. Below are several other helpful examples:

1. In the cooler seasons jackets, hoodies, and such were kept on a hook rack by the door. They would not be forgotten as they were heading out to school and they could easily be hung there upon return. Another saying I once heard--"If you don't throw it down, you don't have to pick it up!"

2. Closet organizers of all sorts can help with reducing clothes clutter.

3. Lunches can be prepared the night before and kept in the refrigerator ready to grab each morning.

4. If lunch is purchased at school, lunch money should be packed away at night or paid online ahead of time.

5. A family calendar hanging in a visible location will also be a true life-saver as the children get older especially if you have children of different ages. We kept ours in the kitchen. This is an organized way to see when and where everyone needs to be so you will not forget games, concerts, appointments, picture day and such. A phone app will work, but it will be even more helpful if all can see the schedules in one place. Remember organization is a mom's friend!

Routine is just as important as organization. Routine helps children of all ages automatically know what to do and what to expect. Regular routine provides help for the parents as well. When there is routine, children develop and grow in the areas of responsibility and independence.

One example of routine that was helpful in our home took place after school. The children would arrive home from school. They would enjoy a snack and then it was right to homework. It was routine. They knew they had to get started and get it done and then they were free to do other things. This helped to make sure that at night or the next morning no one would suddenly remember they needed to complete an assignment. It was done shortly after arriving home from school and settling down. I must add that this is not the same for all children. Some may need a break when they first get home and then later start on any work. The focus is not on when, but rather on a pattern of getting things done so that nothing is forgotten.

Another example of what we did for years was the children always had to select what they would wear to school the next day, the night before. Again, remember easy mornings start at night. This is especially helpful when you have several children of different ages. If older children get in the habit of doing this, you have more time to focus on getting a younger child ready for school. School clothes were ironed and hanging the night before. Church outfits were selected and ready the night before. This was especially helpful with our girls when they got older because they also had to do hair and make-up in the mornings. This was routine for them and even now that they are older, they still make preparations the night before when they have appointments or special places to go. It has become routine for them. It was routine for us to eat dinner together in the evenings. The children when they were younger had a routine bedtime to assure that they got proper rest and it provided down-time for me and my husband. These and many others were areas that allowed the children to know what to do simply because of routines that were established. Routine helped each day run much more smoothly.

Organization and routine both are important. Sure, there are times to break free and enjoy spontaneity. That is fine. Some individuals rather wing it all together and hope that things fall into place daily. Maybe that works, however, if you need help getting to work, worship, appointments, and meetings on time, make organization and routine your friends.

List a few areas that could use organization in your home. Also, list areas where routine would help the day flow more smoothly.

_____

_____

_____

_____

_____

_____

_____

_____

_____

_____

_____

_____

_____

_____

Chapter 6

You're the Mama

This is one of the most important things to remind yourself when you have had a child several years after the older children. If the older children are still in the home, it is often easy to take advantage of the so-called '**built-in-babysitters**'. We heard that term so many times after our younger child was born. Yes, the older children were so much help, but it is important not to allow the weight of the transition to rest on them. You are the mama.

So how do you keep from forgetting that the real responsibility does not rest on the older siblings? Here are two ways that might help you. The first is to make sure that what matters to your older children matter to you. So often the older children get pushed to the back and only the new baby is the focus, especially if the older children are self-sufficient. The second is to enjoy having the so-called 'built-in babysitters', but not to take advantage of them.

Although we had another child almost ten years after our others and she loved hanging with the older children, we made it a priority to give our older children room and space especially as they got to be older teens. They were teenagers driving and participating in many activities. In other words, they had places to go and people to see! We made it a priority to make sure that our having a baby at this stage in their lives would not hinder them from all the things they were a part of. We wanted them to know that they mattered and that we were interested in what mattered to them.

During that time, schedules and routine played even a bigger part in our lives. Our children all participated in high school chorus so we attended many concerts. We had a daughter in band and our son and other daughter were both three sport athletes in high school so our days were filled with band concerts, evenings at chorus concerts, practice drop-offs and pick-ups, and then games, games, and more games.

We and our younger daughter spent many hours on the hard bleachers of basketball games, cold nights by the football field drinking hot chocolate, long weekends at travel volleyball tournaments, hot days in the sun at track meets, Saturday mornings at choir practices and liturgical dance practices, all which was the norm for our younger daughter. She grew up used to rushing here-and-there to support her siblings. These were wonderful family times for us because we spent a lot of time together and all were still able to do the things they loved doing and we supported it all. We did not want our other children to feel that they had to spend their time watching the new baby. They could spend their time doing the things they loved with the full support of their parents. Was it easy? No way but our children could see that what mattered to them would still matter to us even though we were starting over with another child.

Later when our children attended college, there were times when our oldest daughter would visit the middle daughter in college and as much as the youngest wanted to go along, I would find something fun for her to do with my husband and I so the older girls could have time together. Make sure you support what the children are involved in and provide opportunities for the older children to enjoy their activities and times with one another without having to bring the younger child along.

The second thing we did was make a point to raise our younger child and not thrust this responsibility on the children. As I mentioned earlier, our older children were so excited about having a new baby in the family. They held her, fed her, put her to sleep, fussed over who would sit by her in the car and so forth, but it was important that they were not made to feel as if this was their child. As the children got older they did so much for the younger. The girls combed her hair, made breakfast for her, ironed her clothes, and anything else that needed to be done, but they were clear that they were helping because they loved to do it, not because they were made to be the parents. They truly loved it especially as they got older. They were so helpful when my husband and

I would catch a movie or go out of town. The older girls were the "Sistah Mamas" as I called them, and her big brother was her wrestling buddy and great helper as well.

Was every day a perfect day? No not by any means. There were times when the girls would want to go to the mall together and as much as little sister wanted to go along, we would say no. There were times when the older children wanted to watch one thing on TV and the younger child wanted cartoons. There were so many compromises made. We had to use wisdom to make things work in a household with different ages and stages but we made it work.

Keeping the roles clear is important to the love and patience the older siblings will have with the child born much later. Our youngest will grow up with so many memories of dance-offs with the girls, games with her brother, cooking with her sisters, painting nails, doing hair, being spun around in the laundry basket by her brother, and on and on all because the roles were clear and all were shown that they mattered.

The most special times for me have been when the youngest approached nine and ten years old and may have had a hard day or a moment of sadness for some reason. I have seen one of the older sisters pull her aside and talk to her and make her feel better than I or my husband ever could have simply because of the bond and the relationships formed with them all.

You will have many experiences to use as teaching moments for the older children. They can learn responsibility, love, helping others, sacrifice, self-denial and they get to see first-hand just what it took to raise them. Yes, you will have built-in babysitters as many say, but remember they are not the parent, you are the Mama!

List ways you can make sure the
weight of child-rearing does not
rest on your older children.

Chapter 7

The Help is in Your House

L et's face it, when it comes to raising children, things do not always go as planned especially when you find yourself almost done with child-rearing and then starting over. With work, family, many hats to wear, and emotional changes, all the tips in the world may not always help things flow smoothly. When nothing seems to work, remember to keep it simple and ask for help.

Start by getting around those that have accomplished what you are trying to do already. Observe and see if you can glean any tips that will also work for you. Draw from those who have already walked through the season you are in and find encouragement from them.

The help you need may actually be in your house! Remember the organization mentioned in earlier chapters. Keeping organized will help your home and mind stay much clearer. Having places for storage helps to keep things orderly. Your spouse is always a great source of help whether getting things done or taking the younger child out for a bit so that you can get ahead or grab some much-needed rest.

I can remember when our children were younger and I had to lead a regular choir practice each week. My help in the house came in the form of my husband. He was so much help because he would take the children to dinner so that I wouldn't have to cook. They would then go to the park, come home, get baths, and when I arrived home they would all be in the bed asleep. This happened every week. Again, there is that routine we talked about in an earlier chapter. I was able to come home and relax thanks to my help.

Another source of help in the house are the children. I do not mean they are your source of help raising the younger child, but they can provide help for you as it relates to the household. Allowing them to help around the house provides wonderful teaching and training opportunities. I looked for areas that all of the children could help out including the younger one. You may be surprised to know how much personal responsibility they can handle when given the chance. Here are a few examples of things our children did and how children can help around the house:

1. They can make their beds and keep their rooms cleaned which includes putting their dirty clothes in their own hamper.

2. They can load the washing machine and then take clean clothes out of the washing machine and put them in the dryer and separate them when done.

3. Even the youngest can learn to fold towels and small wash cloths.

4. Older children can load and unload dishes from the dishwasher or better yet, hand wash them.

5. Older children can vacuum or sweep and take out the garbage or mow the lawn.

6. They can help with dinner preparation. Our youngest daughter loves to help in the kitchen.

7. They can help care for the family pet.

8. They can help unpack the grocery bags. If they drive, they can run errands.

Simple chores teach children responsibility and they learn the importance of taking care of their surroundings. I cannot promise you that this will carry over into their college dorm rooms, as we now have college students, but I can promise it will help you in your everyday care of child-rearing. These are simple ways to care for the children and still not feel overwhelmed with all that most moms do daily.

List several things around the house that your older/younger children can help do to develop responsibility and provide help for you as well.

Chapter 8

Avoid the 3-C's

One of the biggest mistakes we make as moms is to compare ourselves to others. I once heard a preacher say that he never compares himself to others because either he would leave feeling discouraged if he was not as successful, or he would leave feeling prideful if he had accomplished more. Do not make the mistake of comparing yourself to another mother or another family. Embrace where you are and walk it out. If you are raising a child later in life after your others are older, you cannot look at other couples who seemingly planned well and had the 'one girl/one boy' and no more. They may be traveling and enjoying life while you are still doing back-to-school shopping. Understand that that may not have been the plan for you. Do not compare yourself to others. Instead of feeling down because you are not where they are, think of the woman married for years and not able to conceive. You are blessed because you have more than you expected. Be grateful for your journey and don't compare yourself or your situation to anyone else's. This will shut out discouragement and pride at the same time!

Moms should never compete with others. It happens so often. One family may have their child in violin lessons, gymnastics, art classes and the list goes on and on. Do not give in to the need to fill every day of your week with a mile-long list of activities for your child just because another family does. This will only leave you worn out and tired. Maybe the neighbor got a new family van with stow-and-go seating and you feel you must have a new van as well. No, do not compete with other moms or anyone for that matter. Be confident in who you are. Realize that timing is everything. Know what you need for your family and live within your means. There is no one you need to keep up with. You will find a great sense of peace and contentment in doing so. Embrace your own season and be content.

Lastly, do not over-commit yourself. Learn to just say no. That includes to your children as well at times. I learned quickly after we had our first child, that no one else will respect your time if you do not. My husband and I used wisdom by setting boundaries that protected us as a couple, as parents, and as a family. We made decisions together and prioritized things that would allow us to function as a family. Know what you can and cannot do. Know what your family schedule is and stick to it. Know what the family budget is and stick to it. Your priority is to your family first.

I remember when I had our first child, I was blessed to stay home and raise her. I helped out a few of my friends by caring for their children as well while they worked. However, I had guidelines regarding drop-off times and pick-up times so that I could also be fully present for my own family. It worked out wonderfully. There were organizations and groups that I participated in before having children that I had to step aside from afterwards so that I would not be pulled in so many different directions.

Know what is important for you as a mom so that you do not make the mistake of comparing yourself to others, competing with others, or over-committing yourself. Embrace the stage that you are in knowing that seasons change. You will not always be a mother of small children or a mother of teens. Respect your time, have boundaries in place, and plan your days wisely.

List one of the 3-C's that may have tripped you up and how you can avoid it in the future.

Chapter 9

When All Else Fails

One can have hundreds of tips from every expert there is, however nothing is a guarantee to make every day run perfectly. Yes, there will be days when nothing seems to go right and there may be days filled with total chaos. Don't let this discourage you. If we are not careful, we as moms can be our own worst enemies. We put great demands on ourselves and when they are not met, we are often left feeling overwhelmed. Here are a few final tips that will prove helpful to any mom:

1. Keep it simple. There are times when you should just go with the flow. If a child is sick or for some reason organization, routine, and all else goes out the window, just live! Spontaneity has a way of bringing fresh energy to the mundane. That may mean pizza for a night instead of a hot, home-cooked meal. It may mean everyone digging through the large pile of laundry to find what's needed and organizing it later. Get through the day or the week and start fresh with the next day. It happens.

2. Ask for help. Not only should you use the help in your house, but do not be afraid to ask for help! Take advantage of available help from relatives or those that you trust with your children. It may mean allowing your child to spend a few hours at a relative's home while you and your husband take a night out, or allowing your child to have a play date with another friend to give you a few hours to run errands. Take advantage of good help. I took advantage of good help many times when our older children were all in college and my husband and I needed

to travel or attend some type of event. We were grateful for help with our younger daughter. You will appreciate those that love and respect you and care for your child.

3. Time out! No not for the children, for you the mother. Know when it's time to go. Know when your heart is saying it's time to step away and have a moment for yourself. It's called self-care. It may not mean packing bags and traveling a distance, but it may mean taking a walk, taking a drive, going to a local library for a few moments of peace and quiet, or simply closing the door to your room to relax, pray, or meditate. Whatever the choice is for you, know when to take a time out for yourself. The daily responsibility of raising children is no easy job. Raising another child years after you have raised others is especially no easy job. Over the years of managing a household daily, I found a few things that I liked to do that refresh me. I would take a few hours to visit the spa. I would run out and get a manicure

or pedicure, or take a walk in the fresh air in a local park. Sometimes I would just go for a drive. Identify those things that give you peace and cause you to slow down and refocus. Do those things while someone else helps out with the child or children. Don't forget self-care!

What can you do to simplify your day?

List two people that you love and trust
who you can call on when needing help.

What are a few things you like to do that are peaceful and refreshing for your self-care?

- -

- -

- -

- -

- -

- -

- -

- -

- -

- -

- -

- -

- -

- -

Three Teens and A Toddler Extra Tips

1. Remember that having and raising children is one of the toughest responsibilities yet one of the most rewarding experiences. Enjoy your family.

2. All mothers are working mothers whether in the home or outside of the home and you must know how valuable your role as a mother is.

3. Make time for your spouse. Go on date nights, go out for dinner or breakfast together, take walks in the evenings. Remember one day the children will be 'grown and gone'. Do things to keep your marital relationship strong.

4. Keep balance in your life. Prioritize. Don't sweat the small stuff. No one can do it all and get everything right. Getting it all done is not the priority. The priority is doing what you can and ending each day in a place of peace.

5. Very Important! Do not lose sight of the older children. If your age gap includes a younger child and teens, be sure to keep an eye on the teens as well especially if they are pre-teens or early teens. Know who their friends are, monitor social media and cell phones. Trust me, there will be days when the teens don't mind your focus being all on the new baby or younger child, (wink). However, they still need your guidance and watchful eye.

6. Be aware of major transitions. If your older children are going off to college or marrying and this means the younger child will be home as the only child, give special attention to the younger child during those times. Changes like that can represent major transition for the child left at home. Prepare ahead of time by talking about the

transition, planning play dates and special things to bridge the gap for the younger child. The children can keep in touch through facetime, text, phone calls, etc.

Conclusion

Mothers are valuable and children are the most precious gift that we could ever have. Raising them is one of the most challenging responsibilities, especially if you think you will not have more children and then you find yourself starting over. However, it can be done. My husband and I were determined to put the same energy, time, and fun into raising our child born later just as we did with the others. Yes, it meant back to the park, the pool, the beach, vacations, volunteering at school, silly songs, cartoons, toys, holidays, help with homework, parent/teacher conferences, fieldtrips, teaching Bible stories again, and on and on, but we got it done and so can you. Remember we only have them for a season. Soon they will be adults and moving on with their own lives.

When we were raising our three children who are two years apart, times were challenging but we looked at each stage as a season. That allowed us to enjoy just where they were in life realizing that in just a short time they would be moving on to another stage. We knew that one day we would look back wishing we could have some of those seasons again. So, embrace this time of child-rearing even if it caught you by surprise. With a little planning, preparation, and practical tips you can successfully handle the day-to-day responsibilities of a mom and especially those of a mom raising children with an age gap!

Citations

1   Trop, J. (January 14, 2016) "More Women Over 40 Are Having Babies." *Fortune Magazine*, http://fortune.com/2016/01/14/babies-over-40/

2   Wooller, S. (July 14, 2016) (Updated: July 19, 2016) "New Life Begins At 40." *The Sun Magazine*, https://www.thesun.co.uk/living/1440072/women-over-the-age-of-40-now-giving-birth-to-more-tots-that-those-under-20-for-the-first-time-ever/

Additional Notes:

Additional Notes:

Additional Notes:

Printed in the United States
By Bookmasters